KISSING MAURA O'KEEFFE

Kissing
Maura O'Keeffe

Gerry Murphy

To Conor,

best wishes

Gerry Murphy 20 - 9 - 19

SOUTHWORD*editions*

First published in 2019
by Southword Editions
The Munster Literature Centre
Frank O'Connor House, 84 Douglas Street
Cork, Ireland

Set in Adobe Caslon 12pt

Contents

…holding mary mahony squeezing niamh connolly kissing maura o' keeffe…

As soon as you came in
I wanted to celebrate hugely
I wanted to leap into the small
blue vase and send the daffodils
flying I wanted to prostrate myself
along the bar in homage to your svelte
perfection I wanted to convince the barman
of the absolute significance of the moment
I wanted the Carnival of Rio to emerge
exuberant from the toilet I wanted to invent
vertigo I wanted to exude Revolution
I wanted to sprout red flags I wanted
to bequeath the entire left side of my body
to the people of Leningrad I wanted to depart
there and then for anywhere in Siberia
within warm and easy reach
of your fully extended arms.

That First Kiss

That dazzling afternoon,
our first date culminating
in a precarious kiss
across the glinting handlebars
of your interloping bicycle
under the looming tower
of the University.
A kiss that left
a flurry of indignant muses
flouncing from the Pantheon
in its fizzing wake.
A kiss that wiped them clean
from the dusty archives,
as if they had never been.

Middle age is whispering on Winthrop Street:
"a taxi, a cup of cocoa and then to bed."
A full moon over Marlboro Street
is exhorting me to stay out,
perk up, think nineteen, get a life!
Trees are already stretching into leaf
along the South Mall,
planets are flying wildly past
their preordained perihelia,
bats are fucking frantically in the belfries.
So, I am curling up my toes,
I am sloughing off this ageing skin,
I am kissing Mary Mahony.

Aphrodite Radiant

What if you could go back
to any particular time or place.

Listen again in a tumult of anticipation
for the rumble of her car in the cobbled lane.

The familiar whinge as the rusty gate
scrapes on the concrete path.

The dry squeak of her key in the lock,
her brisk steps clipping up the stairs.

The bustle and flap of discarded clothes
as she undresses on the landing.

And there she is, standing before you,
twenty-three-years-old to the very day.

That glossy black hair, that impish grin,
the *postponer of old* age, incarnate.

On Her Hair
(after the Irish, 15th Century)

Your dark
intricate curls
would put Absalom's
luxuriant but lethal
hair to shame.
In your dusky tresses
a flock of parrots
could nest unnoticed
with a flock of nightingales.
Your perfumed ringlets
invite the bemused poet
to lose himself
and find himself,
then lose himself again.
I could remain
entangled in your
black glossy locks
until Time's
or my own
sorry end.

Rush Hour

I know the pedestrian light
is in your favour
and you must go and go now
but I want to linger
just a little longer in your embrace
at the corner of Washington Street
and South Main Street.
I want to kiss
each individual hair of your head
from root to tip
while the lights change and change again
and the city grinds to a shuddering halt
and the sky tilts over
to reveal teeming constellations,
utterly silent, unbearably distant.

FURTHER OUT

I can't tell you
where this is happening.
I know it's a dream
because the left bank of the Seine
has just appeared directly opposite
the right bank of the Lee.
I know it's daylight,
or at least dream daylight,
that silver-grey, residual glow
from some imploding star
shining in your glossy black hair.
I know it's you
because there is not one
even remotely as beautiful
on the stony inner planets
and I know you have been kissing me
for over a minute
because I have just woken up
gasping for breath.

Ballynoe Haiku

My kisses like bees
in your honey-coloured hair
sweetly mistaken.

Your kisses like rain
on the forgotten desert
of my abdomen.

THE BIG ISSUES

Word comes through
that you are working your ass off.
If there is one as lovely
in the teeming seraglio
of a Turkish soccer player,
I'll eat my fez.
If there are breasts more shapely
beneath the vests
of Mao's fearless militia women,
I'll swallow my little red book.

KISSING MAURA O'KEEFFE

You know thursdays and me
warp nine through the gamma quadrant
to flush dead pigeons from the shuttle-bay
a slow swing around orion to collect
my twenty-nine senses early morning banter
with the milkman the paper boy the post
person farsud zwingli vabblesap beam
down to the uptown grill suck on
burger chips beans sausages mushrooms
and onions tilt full fat face towards
that rare shaft of sunlight glinting off
a wing-mirror dream of holding mary mahony
squeezing niamh connolly kissing maura
o'keeffe somewhere over the rainbow
somewhere over the rainbow my bollocks.

I can't remember what I was looking at
so intently that particular day probably
the cracks in the pavement or those cute
smears of dog-shit which I am convinced
will eventually conform to some quasi-
mystical pattern I have already laid down
in my subconscious and lead to momentary
if ultimately meaningless revelation but
that's another story however I was aware
of that black scarf floating in and out
of my peripheral vision like a remnant
of the last anarchist banner from the last
burning barricade but then I started looking
at you I mean really looking at you head
up straight between those beautiful blue
eyes only to see the enormous sullen
bulk of myself looking back in grim stereo.

So scrap entire physical dimension
all change tear zero back to the future
blueprints under your pillow with assorted
limbs life-support system not to be switched
on until a wave and then another breaking
gently at your feet a scarf wound lightly
about your neck or the hallstand's this
friendship developing still without simple
nourishment will probably lose weight no
problem I can go without holding you easy
don't need so much as want can always hold
myself kiss kiss want to see you though
whatever the arrangement holograms
and tapes if you like hello?

THE EMPTY QUARTER

Where you are tonight
or what you are doing
is immaterial.
In this your tent
is already pitched
at a cool caravanserai
under creaking date-palms.
Your camels are watered, fed, rested
and reciting the secret names of Allah.
You are reclining
in black diaphanous silks
on a jewel-encrusted divan,
where I (in Richard Gere's body)
am kissing you
into a long hot shivering fit.

Rain

Say we went out anyway
under a steady hissing of rain;
say we took the crumbling path
back across the cliffs
above the booming cove;
say we kissed in the periodic glare
from the lighthouse;
say we climbed the ninety-nine steps
to the top of the tower,
undressing as we climbed
and tumbled wet and breathless
onto your welcoming bed;
say you invited me to read
the astonishing astrological predictions
you had had tattooed
on your eloquent skin;
say I am reading still.

Morning In Cefalú

I know
we fell asleep
spooning
but sometime
in the night
you turned
and now I wake
to find you
facing into me,
your forehead
level with my chin,
your breath
damp on my throat.
Lovely as you are,
lulled beyond reach
of the first stirrings
in the morning air,
I cannot help but
kiss you awake.

MUSE

I am writing naked
at the kitchen table
when you steal in
from the shower
and stand on tiptoe
at my shoulder.
A few drops from
your dripping hair
splash onto the lamp-lit page,
blurring the words
I am deploying in your honour.
With an abrupt kiss,
you slip into the bedroom,
your seal of approval
still tingling
from the nape of my neck
down into the small of my back
as I turn the dampened page
and begin again.

CLOSE CALL

I don't know what you were thinking
(actually I do)
pushing me into that doorway,
kissing me into a breathless ferment
and then almost erasing me,
limb by shuddering limb,
with your frenzied frottage.
We were on our way
to the railway station,
you to meet your boyfriend
from the late train,
I to break off long before
and make my way home
without a hint of affection.
Perhaps his train was early
or, more likely,
we had been kissing too long
and too well,
because when we emerged,
flushed, mussed-up and panting
from that feral maul,
he was all but upon us.
I strode on,
dishevelled but purposeful,
towards the station,
you drew him into
your still trembling arms.

MY FLIRTATION WITH INTERNATIONAL SOCIALISM

On Douglas Street
an aromatic Boeuf Bourguignon
is simmering over a low flame
as we walk to the Off-Licence
to choose a sacrificial red.
Near Parliament Bridge,
in a sudden fit of passion,
or simply overcome with hunger,
you kiss the back of my right hand
three times in rapid succession,
taking me totally and delightedly unawares.
That moment of mutual,
wide-eyed affection remains undiminished
through all the elaborate spins
we have subsequently applied
to our brief affair.

The Other Half

Not making love,
lying together
in an embrace
that mat just be
the sweet spot
of all our embraces.
How did we get so *here?*
We dare not stir,
nor try to figure out
the tender mechanics
of how we stumbled
on this makeshift nirvana,
a single breathing entity.
But we do stir
and make love
and lose our place
and haven't found it since.

MATINS

Stop me if I get this right:
It's seven in the morning
on Douglas Street.
I am blundering about the flat,
trying not to wake you,
looking for my keys,
already late for work.
I know I will eventually
have to ask you
and you will tell me
exactly where they are
but for now
I am fumbling through every
pouch and pocket
like a first-time burglar.
Defeated, I stand by the bedside,
steeling myself, preparing to wake you
and suddenly I'm on my knees,
pestering your sweet, sleeping face
with urgent kisses.

LONG SUMMER AFTERNOON

As you sleep,
your tanned pelt
glowing against lemon sheets,
a warm southern wind
whips a sprinkling of rain
through the open window:
A blind cartographer
mapping you with kisses.

In the name of memory,
I claim that quicksilver
trickle of sweat;
its sinuous track
down into the small
of your back;
its slight tickling
at the top
of your buttocks;
its happy drip
into fragrant darkness.

Three days,
two showers later,
your smell fades
from my skin
and I submerge without trace
in the grubby quotidian.
Then, one morning,
several weeks after,
I pull on my grey sweater –
the very one you pressed
into service as a nightgown –
and suddenly inhale you
all over again.

MAYAKOVSKY'S TESTAMENT
(after Stephanie Schwerter)

Our love boat
has run aground
on a sandbar
of the quotidian.
You and I are even.
There is nothing
to be gained
in compiling a list
of our manifest loss.
We loved well,
we parted well,
enough.

PART OF A POEM TO CELEBRATE YOUR NEXT BIRTHDAY

Keeping
one eye open
for
minorfluctuationsinthepropertymarket,
keeping the heart
pent up for Spring,
I watch you swim,
I calculate your trade value.

I could, of course, ask you out:
into the rain forests,
the Jovian ice-fields,
the fresh air?
Onto the lunar surface,
the veldt,
the sea floor?
Is there anything
in particular
you desire?

There's nothing here for you,
at least...
If it's all the same to you...
nothing you could take home
to mother...
I am developing
a fixed obsession
for your navel
...except perhaps
a view of the river
and floating quietly
thereupon...
a small passion for your breasts

...a few dead priests,
though (dare I say it)...
the hots (the very hots)
for your vulva
...(Yes?)
and a cool detached admiration
for your legs...
not enough?

Even if it is
only a matter of days
before the commencement
of nuclear (oh shit) hostilities –
are you digging in
under your Swiss bank account –
and even if Castro is dead –
sorry I mean Lenin –
at least it's Spring
the birds are sing

ing, there is a sharp bluecold wind
streaking in from the Atlantic,
and if you search carefully
along the edge of this poem
or, if you will, along the edge
of the Arctic Circle,
you will find references
to your exquisite face,
the pert delight
of your breasts,
the lovely slow curves
of your hips,
the southern tip
of South America,
that sort of thing.

Of course,
if you are saving yourself
for an Associate Professor
and would rather not
be identified too closely
with this surrealist excess,
lest it be discovered
at some future date
and brought up
before a Senate Sub-committee hearing
on the suitability
of your husband (now a Professor)
as ambassador to Papua New Guinea,
just say so,
I can take a hint.

A Note on The Demise of Communism

I give the Communist salute
to my Capitalist ex-girlfriend
as she takes the corner at a clip
in her black BMW,
doles me out an imperious nod
and leaves me to choke back
Marxist-Leninist rhetoric
in a plume of carbon-monoxide.

Acknowledgements

Some of these poem have appeared in previous collections, namely, *End of Part One,* Dedalus Press 2006, *My Flirtation With International Socialism*, Dedalus Press 2010 and *Muse*, Dedalus Press 2015. My thanks to the Editor of Dedalus Press, Pat Boran.

Printed in Poland
by Amazon Fulfillment
Poland Sp. z o.o., Wrocław